Gallery Books
Editor: Peter Fallon

SIX HONEST SERVING MEN

Paul Muldoon

SIX HONEST
SERVING MEN

Gallery Books

Six Honest Serving Men
is first published
simultaneously in paperback
and in a clothbound edition
on 15 June 1995.

The Gallery Press
Loughcrew
Oldcastle
County Meath
Ireland

ISBN 1 85235 168 3 (*paperback*)
     1 85235 169 1 (*clothbound*)

  The Gallery Press receives financial assistance from An Chomh-
airle Ealaíon / The Arts Council, Ireland, and acknowledges also
the assistance of the Arts Council of Northern Ireland in the publi-
cation of this book.

Characters (*in order of appearance*)

MICK MCCABE, IRA volunteer
SEAMUS MCANESPIE, IRA volunteer
OLIVER CLERY, IRA volunteer
SEAN TAGGART, IRA volunteer
KATE MCINERNEY, widow of Brian McInerney, The Chief
GERRY MCGUFFIN, IRA volunteer
JOE WARD, IRA volunteer

SIX HONEST SERVING MEN
*was originally commissioned and produced
by McCarter Theatre, Princeton, NJ.*

I

Fade up. Dusk. The kitchen of a safe house on the border of counties Armagh and Monaghan, now being used by members of an Active Service Unit of the Irish Republican Army. TAGGART *and* MCANESPIE *are playing cards.* CLERY *is squinting at a book.* MCCABE *has been sitting with his head in his hands. He starts up.*

MCCABE Two weeks, McAnespie. It's been two weeks
since we put that head-the-ball in the ground.
MCANESPIE So what?
CLERY Parnell would have been 'the uncrowned
king of Ireland' had he not dipped his wick
in Kitty O'Shea.
TAGGART 'O shay, can you shee . . .
MCCABE A fortnight since we shouldered his coffin.
TAGGART By the dawn's early light?'
CLERY Where's McGuffin?
MCCABE Char-les Stew-art Head-the-ball.
MCANESPIE BBC. . .
CLERY How do you mean?
MCANESPIE When you say 'had he not'
you sound like some BBC nancy boy.
TAGGART Too right. Like the uncrowned *queen* of The Moy.
MCCABE Where's McGuffin? And where's that other nut?
TAGGART McGuffin and Ward are getting their fill
of baked beans and Marks and Sparks ham and veal.

II

A nearby house on the border of counties Armagh and Monaghan. The table is set for two. KATE *is lounging in an armchair, drinking a gin and tonic. A recording of 'I'll Take You Home Again, Kathleen' is playing on the gramophone.*

'To that dear home beyond the sea,
My Kathleen shall again return,
And when thy old friends welcome thee,
Thy loving heart will cease to yearn.

> KATE *gets up and goes over to the window, peeking out through a corner of a curtain.*

Where laughs the little silver stream,
Beside your mother's humble cot,
And brightest rays of sunshine gleam,
There all your grief will be forgot.

Oh! I will take you back, Kathleen,
To where your heart will feel no pain,
And when the fields are fresh and green,
I'll take you to your home again.'

> *As the song comes to an end* KATE *deftly lifts the arm off the turntable and sets it back to the top of the track.*

III

*A lookout post — little more than a trench with a sod roof — on the
border of counties Armagh and Monaghan.* MCGUFFIN *and* WARD, *who
is peering through a sophisticated night vision scope, are engaged in a
surveillance operation.*

MCGUFFIN Of baked beans and Marks and Sparks ham and veal
washed down with a flagon of Lucozade
I sing.

WARD It's the Marks and Sparks wild locust
and honey pie washed down with rocket-fuel
I'm into myself.

MCGUFFIN You mean 'wild *honey*'.

WARD I mean 'wild *locust*'. I mean camel-hair.
I mean two weeks of breathing the same air
as you, McGuffin.

MCGUFFIN I bet 'Shoshone'
Taggart will shortly be beating a path
to her door. I myself am in no doubt
it was Taggart who had The Chief rubbed out.

WARD I mean a whole two weeks without a bath
except for the time the roof sprang a leak.

> WARD *pulls on a baseball cap which bears the legend*
> 'Stutz Bearcat'.

MCGUFFIN And the sheeted dead did gibber and squeak.

IV

The safe house. A spot that suggests they're being viewed through a night vision scope ranges over TAGGART *and* MCANESPIE *playing cards,* CLERY *reading a book, then comes to rest on* MCCABE, *again with his head in his hands.*

MCCABE   There's something about the way he was hit
that smacks of a set-up . . . An inside job . . .
That's why they're all up to high do.
But what's really put the wind up the rest
of them is that 'Dumdum' Devine and 'Taco' Bell
and Dessie Gillespie haven't come home
for a fortnight. There'll be no light
shed on those three boys till some farmer turns
back into the field to plow the next score
and slices the top off one of their heads.
'And when the fields are fresh . . . ' What is that line?
That's it . . . 'And when the fields are fresh and green.'

V

Kate's house. 'I'll Take You Home Again, Kathleen' is again coming to an end on the gramophone.

> 'Oh! I will take you back, Kathleen,
> To where your heart will feel no pain,
> And when the fields are fresh and green,
> I'll take you to your home again.'

> KATE *again lifts the arm off the turntable with a practised ease, then peeks through a corner of the curtain.*

KATE He always liked that one . . . Chin chin . . .
What he'd do was he'd make the gin
and tonic with the three ice cubes
and one slice of lemon . . . A scoop,
he called it . . . Had to be *one* slice
of lemon . . . And *three* cubes of ice . . .
He'd set the G and T down there
on the arm, so, of the armchair
and close his eyes . . .

> KATE *has sat down in the armchair and closed her own eyes.*

It's not as
if there was anyone but myself
to distract him . . . He closed his eyes,
so, and raised them up to the skies
and every so often he'd smack
his lips . . . His dad heard McCormack
sing this in nineteen-thirty-nine . . .
There were six honest serving men
at the door the very next day
and they put the old boy away
for five years up in Crumlin Road.

When his dad got back he'd read
every book in the library . . .
The Deerslayer and *The Prairie*
and *The Pathfinder* . . . Read them all . . .
The Jungle Book . . . *Puck of Pook's Hill* . . .
To where your heart will find no pain . . .
Your heart was ever fond and true . . .
The Just-So Stories . . . What was it again?
'I keep six honest serving men
(They taught me all I knew) . . . '
He must have learned that from his dad
when he was a lump of a lad
on the Falls Road . . . Gilbey's and Schweppes . . .
The name stuck after a police swoop
when he answered every question
with 'Gilbey': 'Name?' 'Gilbey.' 'Christian
name?' 'Gilbey.' 'Address?' '1-4-0
Gilbey Grove.' 'Ask me no questions, so,'
he'd say, 'and I'll tell you no lies.'
I shut my ears, so . . . Shut my eyes . . .
My mouth . . . Ten years on the dole-queue . . .
I was Mrs Brian Boru . . .
Ten years . . . I can still see the gash
on his head . . . Ten years in Long Kesh . . .
Ten years of riding that old bus
against a stream of shit and piss . . .
Ten years of being met by a tidal
wave of Jeyes Fluid and Dettol . . .
Ten years of playing hide-and-seek
with the screws . . . them spreading the cheeks
of your arse and poking about . . .
Himself and Clery had set out
on another run of the mill
run for the border . . . He was killed
when they stopped for a cup of tea
in Omagh . . .

KATE *gets up and goes over to a small bureau, from which she retrieves an American in-flight magazine. She makes her way back to the armchair, sits down, begins to leaf through the magazine.*

So, now . . . Let me see . . .
There's something in one of these in-flight
magazines that'll throw some light
on all of this . . .

KATE *reads aloud to herself.*

'The illuminated Pepper Mill is anything but "run of the mill". Freshly ground pepper can highlight any meal, especially when dispensed with this unique illuminated pepper mill. Gourmet peppercorns are freshly ground at the touch of a finger, while a built-in light shines on the peppering area. Add a touch of brilliance to dinner. Batteries included.'

It was 'Taco' who brought this back
from the States . . . Brought back a whole stack
of these buck-stupid magazines . . .
'Taco' himself hasn't been seen
or heard of for ages . . . It's been two weeks
without as much as a dicky-bird's squeak.

VI

The safe house.

CLERY And all the while the sheeted dead did squeak
and gibber in the cages of Long Kesh,
the walls of which they'd smeared with their own keek.
MCANESPIE Nancy boy.
CLERY   I can still see the huge gash
in his forehead.
MCCABE   That bloody head-the-ball.
MCANESPIE Shut up, Mugabe. If it's all the same
to you . . .
TAGGART (*Mockingly*) Two weeks since we six bore his pall.
MCANESPIE I'd as soon have no truck with foreign games.
MCCABE Come again?
MCANESPIE   'Head-the-ball.' That's from soccer.
TAGGART Whoever it was double-crossed The Chief
will be toodling back for another feel . . .
CLERY Of Our Lady of Perpetual Succour.
TAGGART And when she has his bit between her teeth
(TAGGART *puts his right index finger to his mouth*)
hail and farewell . . .
CLERY   *Ave atque vale.*

VII

Kate's house.

KATE 'Chart your destination with information from beyond earth. The Panasonic KX-G5500 Global Positioning System Receiver (GPS) is an amazing navigational tool that helps guide you to your destination.'

VIII

The lookout post.

MCGUFFIN In the last volume of *Hail and Farewell*
Moore describes Yeats coming back from the States
with a pot-belly. All our troubles date
from when Taggart came back from Somerville . . .

WARD With a pot-belly?

MCGUFFIN   No. With a swelled head.
His head and his dick are both two sizes too big.
I swear I heard her squealing like a pig
last night.

WARD   That *was* a pig.

MCGUFFIN   What's that you said?

WARD That *was* a pig.

MCGUFFIN   Since 'Shoshone' came back
from his little shopping trip in Boston
they always seem to know our position
when we go to launch a mortar-attack.

WARD Whatever he might be, he's not a grass,
though he sure as hell does talk through his ass.

IX

Kate's house.

KATE 'Say "Hello" in a voice your mother won't recognise. The Digital Voice Changing Telephone allows you to program 16 different voice levels. Changes your voice from male to female, female to male, adult to child or child to adult.'

X

The lookout post. A spot suggesting that they are themselves under surveillance through a night vision scope ranges over the sleeping MCGUFFIN, *coming to rest on* WARD.

WARD   As for Taggart, there'd be wigs on the green
        if he knew who'd been hammering a job
        on Kate . . . He has a bit of a swelled head,
        for sure, but he's never been one to rest
        on his laurels . . . He wanted us to turn
        'professional' . . . To give up those rickety home-
        made bombs for off-the-peg, top-of-the-line,
        high-tech stuff . . . That wasn't such a great hit
        with The Chief . . . He didn't care if we scored
        the odd own-goal . . . He liked old-fashioned
          'derring-do' . . .
        Shot and shell . . . Forward, the Light
        Brigade . . . Hero fell . . . Mouth of hell . . . 'Taco' Bell.

XI

The safe house.

TAGGART The Chief sure as hell did talk through his ass.

MCANESPIE Once you plaster your walls with your own doo
people start to pay attention to you,
he did know that.

CLERY *'And Parnell loved his lass.'*

TAGGART You understand that too, don't you, McCabe?

MCANESPIE He knew that if you go on hunger strike
you're taking your finger out of the dyke.

TAGGART Don't you, Mugabe?

MCANESPIE Like that wee, Dutch cub
who saved his country with his forefinger.

CLERY *'And Parnell loved his country.'*

TAGGART Loved his *cunt.*

MCANESPIE The emotional tide ...

MCCABE Connolly. Ceannt.

TAGGART That Kitty. Must be a real humdinger.

MCCABE Clarke. MacDonagh. Pearse.

MCANESPIE The tide it released
was incredible.

TAGGART That's some shopping list.

XII

Kate's house.

KATE 'Grundig's Traveller II brings you a world of news and entertainment over five short-wave frequencies and lets you tune in to local FM stereo or AM stations whether you're at home or abroad. Dual time function displays the time in two separate time zones — ideal for international travel. Humane Wake System starts low and gets progressively louder. Includes earbud headphones, frequency guide and carrying case.'

XIII

The lookout post.

MCGUFFIN In-cre-di-ble. We heard Chopin and Liszt
in the Ulster Hall. After '68
and '69, that was completely lost.

WARD Civil Rights?

MCGUFFIN Burntollet Bridge. The Bogside.
I dropped out of Queen's after my first term.

WARD 'Tune in, turn on, drop out.'

MCGUFFIN It was Clery
who introduced me to magic mushrooms.

WARD Rocket-fuel.

MCGUFFIN 'Doctor Timothy' Clery,
he called himself.

WARD He's a spoilt bloody priest.
The only thing worse than a sky pilot
is one who never won his wings.

MCGUFFIN He'll pass.

WARD You think so?

MCGUFFIN Just look at the night they burst
in on The Chief and shot him in cold blood.
He managed to get past the SAS.

XIV

Kate's house.

KATE 'The world changes, and this magnetic puzzle globe changes right along with it. A worldwide success invented and developed in Canada, this is the only globe you'll ever need. Discover the world piece by piece, with the 470 durable pieces which interlock to form an accurate, to-scale representation of the world. Each piece depicts a state, country, province or region. As the world changes, so does the Magnetic Globe. Details on political/geographical update pieces will accompany your purchase. Keep the old pieces for historical reference and rebuild the world as it was in any given year.'

XV

The safe house.

CLERY I'd never have got past the SAS
had I not climbed up into the attic
of the house in Omagh.

TAGGART When they attacked
what was the first thing you heard?

MCANESPIE Breaking glass?

MCCABE Maybe somebody shouted a warning?

CLERY The first thing? I suppose it was Gilbey
screaming, *'Mea culpa, mea culpa . . .'*
And I remembered those Sunday mornings
when we were . . . We were on the altar . . .
'Me a cowboy, me a cowboy,' he'd say,
'me a . . .'

TAGGART You had time to get all the way
up the stairs and then up . . . What? A ladder?

CLERY You should be in Castlereagh, with your fist
down the throat of some bloody terrorist.

XVI

Kate's house.

KATE 'The ancient way of telling time now becomes the state of the art. The Digital Sand Timer executive desk clock features a count-down and count-up timer and alarm clock. Sixty digital "grains of sand" fall to the bottom each minute. Return to the clock feature by simply pressing the button. Can be used as an alarm clock and count-down timer with buzzer. Two button cell batteries included. Black.'

XVII

The safe house. The spot ranges over CLERY, MCCABE *and* TAGGART, *coming to rest on* MCANESPIE.

MCANESPIE When Michael Collins' time ran out at Béal
na mBláth it should have meant the end of the line
for the ballot-box, since the Armalite
and the Armalite alone will hit
the Brits where it hurts . . . It all has to do
with settling a six hundred year old score . . .
Simple as that . . . Brits Out . . . Yankee Go Home . . .
'Four Green Fields' and 'The Wearin' of the Green' . . .
The Chief looked more like the Shroud of Turin
than your usual, your average, wet job . . .
He looked calm . . . Like he was somehow at rest
even though he was missing half his head.

XVIII

The lookout post.

WARD   Down his own bloody throat . . . They found him trussed like a Moy Park chicken with his bollocks stuffed down his own throat like a bloody plug.

McGUFFIN   Like a dressed pig. Odd, that. How they say 'dressed' . . .

WARD   McAnespie's convinced the UVF . . .

McGUFFIN   When they mean '*un*dressed'.

WARD   Were in on the job with the SAS.

McGUFFIN   Why?

WARD   They like to chop off dicks. In fact, they *love* to chop them off.

McGUFFIN   That they do. Then there's them that love to set a wee bit of a — you know? — booby-trap.

WARD   Taggart?

McGUFFIN   'Shoshone' came back from his trip with the makings of . . .

WARD   They call 'Lucozade' '*Gator* . . .

McGUFFIN   A smart bomb . . .

WARD   . . . ade'.

McGUFFIN   No more diggers. No more rockets launched from double-deckers.

XIX

The safe house. The spot ranges over CLERY, MCCABE *and* MCANESPIE,
coming to rest on TAGGART.

TAGGART   I suppose things really came to a head
in the old land of the free and the home
of the brave . . . I was in 'The Rebel's Rest'
on Christmas Eve when they nabbed me . . . No green
card? Huh. Three of them. One looked like Oddjob.
A Magnum? Huh. Five years . . . If I'd, huh, turn
Queen's Evidence? I knew it . . . Knew the score
immediately . . . Jingle Bells . . . Jingle Bells . . .
We jingled all the way out to Brookline
and I sat there at some Christmas Eve do
listening to Perry Como's 'Greatest Hits'
and getting completely wasted on Amstel Light.

XX

Kate's house.

KATE 'What is every crossword puzzler's dream come true? The Crosswords Puzzle Solver from Franklin. Just type in the letters you know and a question mark for the ones you don't. In seconds, Crosswords gives you the answer from a 250,000 word list that includes famous people, cities, sport teams, national parks, inventors, flowers, cooking items and more. It will even finish phrases when only part of the phrase is known.'

XXI

The safe house.

MCCABE   Dessie Gillespie?

TAGGART   That's Desmond Deck'er
to you.

MCANESPIE   Liked to open up the missus
of a Saturday night.

MCCABE   Dicky ticker?

TAGGART   The very one. It always amazes
me when I think of the number of times
they opened him up.

MCCABE   A triple by-pass?

TAGGART   The *Hillsborough* by-pass.

MCANESPIE   Him and 'Dumdum'
and 'Taco' Bell, they say, were on the piss
in McSorley's with a few of the lads
two Saturdays ago . . .

CLERY   Get to the point,
McAnespie.

MCANESPIE   The point is these two boys
came in and started acting the bin lid.

CLERY   You don't say?

MCANESPIE   Someone rammed a bayonet
up Dessie's ass. Next stop was . . .

MCCABE   Aughnacloy.

XXII

Kate's house.

KATE 'The hiker's dream. Add a new dimension to your hiking or climbing experience with Avocet's Vertech Alpine. This revolutionary wrist instrument quantifies your hiking and climbing effort. It documents your progress by automatically accumulating the total vertical feet you climb or descend in a day, week or year. The Vertech measures altitude up to 60,000 feet in ten-foot increments with aircraft altimeter technology, and it tells you how fast you're climbing by displaying current, maximum and average vertical rates of ascent.'

XXIII

The lookout post.

MCGUFFIN You should have seen the cut of Aughnacloy
after the last delivery of Tate
and Lyle.
WARD Most of it was in the Free State,
I'll bet.
MCGUFFIN Five hundred pounds.
WARD Five hundred troy
or avoirdupois?
MCGUFFIN That icing sugar
and diesel mix still packs a powerful punch.
Since 'Shoshone' got back . . .
WARD Back with the paunch?
MCGUFFIN He's become such a mover and shaker
it makes me sick.
WARD It *is* his 'area of expertise',
as he puts it.
MCGUFFIN Don't you find it even
remotely odd that at half eleven
the same night Taggart's 'flying burritos'
were found . . .
WARD They were found? Found by who?
MCGUFFIN By
whom?
WARD By *who?*
MCGUFFIN The Chief was rubbed out in Omagh.

XXIV

Kate's house.

KATE 'The ability to see at night has long eluded mankind. The Nightmaster Second Generation Night Vision Scope changes all that. Our unique hand-held night observation scope magnifies ambient starlight to enhance your natural vision by over twenty thousand times. An admirable tool for turning night into day.'

XXV

The safe house.

TAGGART The night the Chief was rubbed out in Omagh
Dessie and 'Dumdum' and . . .

CLERY   Dirty tricks . . .

TAGGART Had been taken to Aughnacloy by six
honest serving men . . .

MCANESPIE   Six bloody homos . . .

TAGGART From the Queen's Own . . .

MCANESPIE   Queers . . .

TAGGART   They were no
sooner
arrested and placed under detention
than they were out again.

MCANESPIE   With a pension.

CLERY McGuffin will tell you . . .

TAGGART   I set a snare
on the hill the other day.

CLERY   He'll confirm
that he and I were up in Donegal . . .

MCCABE Where in Donegal?

CLERY   Moville.

TAGGART *has put on his coat and moves towards the
door.*

TAGGART   Just dangle
a bit of wire . . .

MCCABE   Moville?

CLERY   Moville . . . A farm
owned by a cousin, I think, of Deck'er's.

TAGGART *opens the door and leaves.*

TAGGART It's time to see if I've any takers.

XXVI

The lookout post. The spot passes over WARD, *asleep, settling on*
MCGUFFIN.

MCGUFFIN Two weeks of this elaborate starlight
while we wait to see who's going to score
with Kate . . . Who cares about who's going to hit
her jackpot? Who cares who rings her bell?
It's a smokescreen . . . Who cares who's doing a line
with Kate McInerney? That 'Kate-man-du',
as Clery calls her . . . Kate would do a turn
with a pot-bellied pig . . . She'd give head
to a dead horse . . . She'd give a dog a blow-job . . .
All changed . . . Changed from the time
I took her home myself . . .
Changed utterly . . . Wherever green . . .
Whereon 'twere best my eyes should never rest.

XXVII

Kate's house.

KATE 'Chart your destination with information from beyond earth. The Panasonic KX-G5500 Global Positioning System Receiver (GPS) is an amazing navigational tool that helps guide you to your destination. Capable of tracking from five satellites simultaneously, it gives you three dimensional positioning for marine, avionic and terrestrial use. This hand-held unit provides latitude, longitude, altitude, date, local or universal coordinate time, speed over ground, estimated time en route and estimated time of arrival. Programmable up to 99 waypoints. One year warranty.'

XXVIII

The lookout post.

MCGUFFIN   It all came from Rabindranath Tagore,
that mystical thing in him . . . A mix
of Tagore and Blake.

WARD   That puts a tiger
in your tank alright.

MCGUFFIN   Just how much Semtex
did we lose?

WARD   Lose where?

MCGUFFIN   Outside of Tempo.

WARD   Five hundred pounds.

MCGUFFIN   Why risk using diesel
and icing sugar when he had a dump
with enough Semtex . . . ?

WARD   'An t-Iompodh Deiseal.'

> MCGUFFIN *peers intently through the night vision scope.*

MCGUFFIN   You what?

WARD   Tempo . . . Turning towards the sun . . .
That's what it means.

> MCGUFFIN *passes the scope to* WARD.

MCGUFFIN   What does *this* mean, *a stóir*?

WARD   Who is it?

MCGUFFIN   He just couldn't keep his paws
off the honey-pot . . .

> WARD *passes the scope back to* MCGUFFIN.

WARD   He must be insane.

MCGUFFIN   He's looking up here . . . He's knocking the door.

WARD   I can't believe it's *that* bloody keogh-boy.

XXIX

Kate's house. There are three knocks on the door. KATE *quickly returns the in-flight magazine to the bureau. She peeks through the curtain, then quite collectedly goes to the door, opens it, and gives a smile of recognition.*

XXX

The safe house.

CLERY Is your head cut? You let *both* Mugabe
and Taggart go? Is your head bloody cut?

MCANESPIE You listen to me, Clery, you hoor's git.
Mugabe spent six years in the same kip
as The Chief. They were both on the blanket.

CLERY And once Mugabe got out of the Kesh
he was *under* the blanket...

MCANESPIE   Hold your wheesht...

CLERY Along with Pearse, Joseph Mary Plunkett,
Connolly, Clarke, Ceannt — and maybe Clark Kent
and Lois Lane — as well as Kiss Me Kate.

MCANESPIE That's sacrilege, Clery. I swear to God
I'll personally cut off your gonads
and stuff them down your throat.

CLERY   I'll have to hum
along to the tune of 'I'll Take You Home...'

XXXI

Cross fade to Kate's house. 'I'll Take You Home Again, Kathleen' is once more playing on the gramophone. KATE *is seeing her visitor out the door.*

> 'Oh! I will take you back, Kathleen,
> To where your heart will feel no pain,
> And when the fields are fresh and green,
> I'll take you to your home again.'

> *As the song comes to an end* KATE *gets up and, deftly as ever, lifts the arm off the turntable.*

KATE Taggart came back . . . himself and 'Taco' Bell . . .
with this unbelievable pile
of magazines . . . How to hunt ducks . . .
How to shoot deer . . . Deadfalls . . . Decoys . . .

> *The phone rings.* KATE *goes to answer it.*

All that stuff . . . 'Taco' drank porter
all night, I'd say, then ran for the border
as usual . . .

> KATE *picks up the phone.*

> Hello . . . (*Pause*) Hello . . .

> KATE *puts down the phone.*

It's them shites
from M15 . . . Them and their satellites . . .

> KATE *goes over to the window, pulls back curtain, calls out.*

Scumbags . . . Dickheads . . . Cocksuckers . . .
(*Aside*) I learned that from the Bon Secours
Sisters . . . (*Loudly*) You wanna see my tits?

    KATE *moves away from window, returns to the arm-*
    chair, picks up her gin and tonic.

At least six months ago it hit
me the phone was tapped . . . I could smell
the fuckers . . . Next thing 'Taco' Bell
told me how both 'Dumdum' Devine
and himself heard clicks on the line
when they picked up . . . Though Taggart knew
about it, he told me to say and do
nothing . . . Thy loving heart will cease to yearn . . .
My Kathleen shall again return . . .
Suppose the men I took into my bed
would take it then into their heads
to give Gilbey the chop . . .
Suppose they're doing a snow-job
on me with their fawning, fulsome
flattery . . . All taking me home
like they took Dessie home . . . I mean
pointing to chapter and verse in The Green
Book while poking him in the chest
with butts and matches and the rest . . .
For I can't believe Dessie's done a bunk . . .
I can't believe he's lying drunk
in a ditch like Puck of Pook's Hill . . .
Lord *Muck*, more like, of *Clabber* Hill . . .
'I keep six honest serving men
(They taught me all I knew);
Their names are What and Why and When
And How and Where and Who.'
Dessie Gillespie would have found
his way back unless he was bound
and gagged, so, and thrown down a well . . .
There's no way he's alive and well

after a two week long bender . . .
Dessie Gillespie, *Pathfinder* . . .

> KATE *goes back to the bureau, retrieves the in-flight*
> *magazine, leafs through it, finds what she's looking*
> *for.*

There's simply no way he's alive . . .
(*Reads*) 'Capable of tracking from five
satellites sim-ul-tan-e-ous-ly . . . '
Home of the brave . . . Land of the free . . .

> KATE *sets aside the magazine.*

Then McCabe rides out of the west
to tell me I'll be under house-arrest
until further notice . . . There are two churns
set in that gap where the Brits sometimes turn
their jeeps . . . Blow you to smithereens,
those churns . . . Forty shades of *gang*rene . . .
'Don't bother,' he says, 'with the shed . . .
Don't bother your pretty little . . . '
Don't bother my arse . . . Me that ran comms
from Long Kesh? Me that left the British Home
Stores an extra half-pound of chip-
olatas, so, in which I'd done my job . . .
Don't bother me with all that ballyhoo
when I know full well they're planning to do
in Clery . . . Just because I'm half-tight
doesn't mean I can't see it's lights
out for that pair who joined in '69 . . .
Clery and McGuffin . . . They wouldn't toe the line . . .
For even if I am half-tore
I know that Ward will want to score
a hat-trick and send 'Shoshone' to hell
in a handbasket . . . Ding dong bell . . .
What use has McCabe for the bit
of a Black & Decker . . . ? And, come to think of it,

what use has Ward for Paraquat?
Why does his hat say 'Stutz Bearcat'?
When was he out in Omaha?
How can he tell Daz from Omo?
Where will he launch his SAM?
Who's gonna take *that* motherfucker home?

XXXII

The safe house. The spot ranges over MCANESPIE, *settling on* CLERY.

CLERY McGuffin will tell them . . . He'll never rest
until my name is cleared . . . It was my turn
to drive The Chief to a farm up near Green-
castle . . . Somewhere on Inishowen Head . . .
It was Taggart's idea we stop in Omagh
to fine-tune the plans for another job . . .
Next thing I knew there was this whole to-do
with a half-division, it seems, of light
artillery . . . That I came through the line
of fire unscathed was, in a sense, to score
a hit, a very palpable
hit . . .

XXXIII

The lookout post.

WARD Look here. You don't have to be Sherlock Holmes
to see that Mugabe had the motive
to kill The Chief.

MCGUFFIN   Not the *loco*-motive . . .

TAGGART *appears from nowhere, brandishing an auto-
matic pistol which he aims at* MCGUFFIN.

TAGGART Too right. He hasn't what it takes to aim
a pistol at somebody's head and shoot.
He's too full of shit. 'How are things with Che
Guevara?' 'The terrorist of today
is the statesman of tomorrow.' That shit . . .
McCabe is counting on the crock of gold
at the end of the rainbow. It's a crock
of shit.

WARD   Go easy on him.

TAGGART   How's the crack
up here, Joe?

WARD   Not bad.

TAGGART   Still packing the Colt?

WARD Could be.

TAGGART *swings round and aims at* WARD.

TAGGART   Any more of your bloody cheek
and I'll blow both of you into next week.

XXXIV

Kate's house. KATE *sings along to the final verse and chorus of 'I'll Take You Home Again, Kathleen', which is once again playing on the gramophone.*

KATE 'Where laughs the little silver stream,
Beside your mother's humble cot,
And brightest rays of sunshine gleam,
There all your grief will be forgot.

Oh! I will take you back, Kathleen,
To where your heart will feel no pain,
And when the fields are fresh and green,
I'll take you to your home again.'

Just as the song comes to an end two pistol shots are heard in the distance. KATE *puts her right index finger to her mouth in a gesture reminiscent of Taggart's in Scene VI. The record continues to grate and grind.*

XXXV

Cross fade FX. The safe house. MCCABE *enters.*

MCCABE   Two weeks, McAnespie. It's been two weeks
of baked beans and Marks and Sparks ham and veal
while the sheeted dead did gibber and squeak,
'Hail and farewell'.

MCANESPIE   Not 'Moville'. 'Emyvale'.

MCCABE   You sure?

MCANESPIE   Sure.

CLERY   You're talking through your ass
if you think I'd shop you.

MCANESPIE   We have a list
we happened to get past the SAS.

MCCABE   From our own 'Deep Throat'.

MCANESPIE   Tie him by his wrists
and hand me over that Black & Decker.

> MCCABE *binds* CLERY's *wrists and rummages about the
> room.*

CLERY   Please, McCabe.

MCANESPIE   You were seen in Aughnacloy
at the time The Chief was killed in Omagh.

CLERY   Says who?

MCANESPIE   Tiger.

> MCCABE *has uncovered a power drill. He brings it to*
> MCANESPIE.

CLERY   Me a . . .

MCCABE   Who's this Tiger?

MCANESPIE   The point is . . .

CLERY   Me a . . . Mexican cowboy.

MCANESPIE *flicks a switch on the drill. It begins to turn, its sound amplified and mixed with the record's grating and grinding.*

MCANESPIE The point is . . . The point must be driven home.

XXXVI

Cross fade to Kate's house. KATE *is standing by the window, as if in shock. She barely registers the entry of* WARD, *who goes over to the gramophone and, with a gesture almost as practised as her own, lifts the arm from the turntable.* WARD *then goes to the armchair and sits down. He picks up the in-flight magazine and begins to leaf through it.*

WARD These airline magazines are full of shit . . .

        KATE *turns from the window.*

KATE   You've hit
the nail on the head there, Joe . . .

WARD   Ambient starlight . . .
An admirable tool, Katie . . .

        KATE *moves towards* WARD *as if in a trance.*

KATE   Ding dong *bell,*
the cat is in the well . . .

WARD 'When you come home, put your feet up and have a
     rest . . . '

KATE Who put her in?

WARD   McCabe worked for Securicor . . .

KATE (*Angrily*) McCabe was in-fucking-terned . . .

WARD   What's
this 'jojoba'?

KATE Who put him in?

WARD   'Jojoba'.

KATE (*Correcting his pronunciation*) Jojoba . . . Little Johnny
     Green.

        KATE *turns away from* WARD. *Fade out.*